Were you there?

Vietnam Notes:
Birth
Death
Infinity

Wayne "Randy" Cribbs Viet Nam 66–67
Illustrated by Matt Cribbs

Published by OCRS, Inc.

Library of Congress Control Number: 2002114651

ISBN 0-9725796-0-5

Typesetting: Publishing Professionals, Port Richey, FL

Illustrations: Matt Cribbs

Printed by: United Graphics

Printed in the United States of America

**To obtain more copies of this book, go to
www.somestillserve.com**

Table Of Contents

Duffel Bag   48–66

Things in Our Head   67–84

Back Home   85–92

Bad Things   93–108

Not All Bad   109–123

Finally   124–130

The greatest tragedy is war,
But so long as there is mankind,
There will be war.
–Jomini
The Art of WAR

For My Brothers

And Their Loved Ones

"Allons"

Bonds

Without thought or will
The bond between fellow
   Warriors grew tight,
Mysteriously intertwined
With a fear of growing too close,
Knowing some would be lost
   In the fight.

Too benign for macho youth
Those expressions of caring
   That ran so deep;
Taught too young to
Hold a gun,
And too early not to weep.
Reluctantly, we came there
In innocent youth,
   Sharing destiny with our brother,
Learning quickly we
   Had only each other.

Now, all these years
Later, surrounded by
The trappings of life,
Far removed from
   That surreal strife,
Even now,
   Only we truly understand
   Those bonds forged so
   Deeply, in that place,
      In that strange land.

About That Place

Path

So patient,
Secure in the belief
That we too would depart,
Like all those before,
Leaving barely a mark.
The jungle now
Not so lush,
   More of a hush,
Not so many creatures
On its soft ground.
The path, their path,
Still there,
Waiting,
Just more wear,
But tolerant of strangers tread
Carrying away their dead
   To never return,
   No more to learn.
Patience rewarded,
With some cost
For all those lost;
But the path as beautiful
As the first time passed,
Knowing
The last time
   Was not the last.
So familiar, so faithful
Down this trail,
With ease, where
We stumbled, fell;
Where they could see
   So well
In this place to us,
   So much hell.

Mystery Land

This land
Lush and green,
Sometimes shimmering
From that mixture
Of light and wet,
Now dry, layered
With fine dust,
Choking and stinging.

Which are you,
So primitive
Yet so full of allure
With your colored birds
And great beasts
And patient children
Who weep real tears,
In vain
   For this place tortured,
    Once again.

Curtain

The jungle night,
So dark
I
Float into it,
Enveloped
  By black space,

At the mercy of
Whatever is within,
  Unseen.

The sky
Hidden,
Somewhere
In my
Sixth sense;

Up is assumed,
  Uncertain,
Direction transcended
By that soft dark curtain.

Lull

The jungle sunrise.

Amplified by light
Shimmering across a
Neighboring rice paddy.

Dark shapes not yet
Recognizable appear
Unreal, ghostlike.

Tranquil.

So calm,
It makes the
Fight to come seem
More sinister than
wounds that will
Surely follow out of the
Noise and smoke
That has no place here.

Counterpart

Viet cong, chuck,
Charlie;
 VC..
So many names for
The counterpart of me.
Some names
Way off the mark
For these little men
Moving silently in the dark.
Mr. Charlie, more
Fitting than dink or gook;
They owned the land,
We had only what was stuck
 To our boot.
Their crime,
These peasants from another time,
Part of the red scourge
Or so we have heard.
Resting quickly, quietly,
In some gentle breeze,
Squatting, arms
Around bony knees,
Then moving again,
Off into the dark,
Mr. Charlie,
With all that heart.

Charlie

Creeping about at night
In our ears, but not sight,
Noise left, rustle right,
Peer with all your might;
   Maybe it's Charlie.
Quietly, without effort,
Oblivious to the hurt,
Black shirt
Be ever alert;
   It's probably Charlie.
Trip flare,
Prickly hair,
Who will scare?
   Not Charlie.
No smoke,
No spark,
For he's there
In the dark.
   Charlie.

Little Man in Black

Minutes ago, my enemy;
Probably neither of us knew why.
Just two soldiers trying to survive,
   And it was he to die.

Strange that I feel sad
For this little man in black,
Just another number
In the body count,
   Added to the stack.

But I do mourn him
As I hope others will,
And pray he is at heavens door;
This little man in black
   Is my enemy no more.

Bunker

So loud the rain.

But in my room
Of sand and wood,
  Secure, blissful refrain.

Flares through a
Continual mist
Floating, lost,
Hazy,
Like falling stars,
  Now like a cross.

White, red, green,
A rainbow in the
Wet sky, burning
In defiance
Of monsoon,
Burning for me,
Secure

In my room...

Monsoon

No rest at all
As the rain begins to fall;

Such a strange pain,
Its' wetness,
The roaring refrain.
We are like a worm,
Hooked to twist and squirm.

To be dry, find a way,
No sleep, wherever you lay.
Boot gripping mud,
Every downpour a flood,
Red dirt cratered like
  The moon
By the torrent that
  Is monsoon.

Wet

Of the many things you
Can loathe about this land,
With its' primitive jungles,
Mud, dust, and sand,
One is surely that
When it is wet
You cannot stay dry,
No matter how hard you try,
And when it's dry,
You are still wet,
Only now from your own sweat.

Monsoon leaves you
Longing to be dry,
Though when the rains stop,
   You wonder why.

Predictable weather, the
Kind you love to hate,
Controlled by forces unknown,
Pre-determined by fate.

Give me dry, should I be
Allowed to choose,
Then at least it's
My sweat to lose.
On second thought,
Is hot better than wet?
   YOU BET!

Tethered

Those great steel
Rumbling beasts
Belching smoke as
Black as the jungle night,
Shattering the quiet,
As all living things
   Take flight.

They are our horses,
Cold and hard, powerful
When ground fits tread
And those great guns
Spit their lead.
But
Soon, no rumble, no boom;
For today comes the tether
   Of monsoon.

Before and After

Surely a mistake has been made.
This jungle floor was not intended
For pits and craters, broken blades,
machines to confuse
   Its creatures.

This primitive place,
Serene,
And us, unwelcome guests
Depriving all within
   Of rest.
Will we remember
Sucking its' life out
Just
As fire dwindles
To embers.

Will a new wind blow
To restart the flame,
To make this place
As before we came.

19

Water Buffalo

Tractors of that primitive place.
Sloshing through paddies,
Up dykes, where no
Steel beast could go.
Powerful, yet moved
At the bidding of tiny
Children.

Doing the work of
Many with
Fierce loyalty, seeking
Little in return.
Simplicity in its
Purest form, measuring
Each day in paces, yoked
But full of pomp, as
If knowing it could
   Be the conqueror.

Kids

Dark smiling eyes.
Smiling, no matter what.
Faces engraved with
   Anxiety,
Not expressive,
   But smiling.
Facing the wide glare
Of another day,
Hands out,
Grateful when filled,
   Rewarded with a smile.

Even as smoke darkens
The sky,
Shelter and rice gone,
To deprive those we sought,
Even then,
   Smiling;
As if not knowing what
Else a child could do.
   Their defense
   Against the others;
   And us, their saviors.

The Job

Night patrol

Final checks of the
Ornaments that adorn
  A warrior.
Jesters grow quieter,
  More subdued,
Mind shifting to the
Business at hand,
Into the cruelty of silence;

Transition to that doubtful
Time between night and day,
Hide and seek among
Natures' offerings—
Time to play.
Rising in unison,
On cue,
Like a debt that must
Be paid when due.

Filing out into the
Hands of fate
Where chance is
Only another alternative
Lying in wait,
then limping home again
as light splinters through trees,
Beyond harms reach.
  The unspoken prayer of each..

Night Enemy

Through the night nothing stirred;
Pleasing to the ear, nothing heard.

They come in the dark
Leaving barely a mark,
Slipping through shadows hidden,
Guests unbidden.

But not this night,
Now giving way to light.
So rest easy, you may;
   Soon comes the day..

Mortar Crew

So reassuring
Hearing them work,
   That mortar crew.
Not many words,
But they knew.

Rounds passing hand to hand;
Metallic,
Thump,
Brief silence,
A roar from the other end.

The more rounds out
The better for that crew;
Less to carry, with
Each puff of smoke, pale blue.

That lethal little tube,
Slinging death so far,
And oh, so much better
Here with the thump than
   Where those other guys are.

Outgoing

Red trail in
The night,
Tracers from the
Rifle recoiless
On my right,
Shrieking back
At the challenge,
Seeking a mark,
Somewhere,
Out there
   In the dark.

Mortar rounds;
One hanging,
Two hanging,
Quietly dropped to land
   Where I cannot see.
Deafening; will I
Ever hear again
In this life—short
   Though it may be.

The Job

Into the Night

Peering into the night,
Nothing there, or
Maybe
Just beyond my sight.

That feeling like a cold dark storm
Closing around.
Too dark, too quiet,
No sound;
Radioman, illumination round.

A low whistle overhead
And the night burns;
Movement, crouching,
Eerie shadows;

Worst fears confirmed.

ARVN

The ARVN did
Not always stay;
Never a surprise when
Smoke cleared and
They had run away;
Maybe nothing new
To them—who can say;
Better to live
And fight another day.

It is not for me to scold,
My lot has always
    Been overbold.
And too, for them,
That insane situation
Was their life,
And we, just another
Group, full of advice;
Clearly they had learned
None of us live twice.
Twelve months and we were done.
No need to run
When the end is in sight,
Easier to stay and fight.

But the ARVN, day after day,
Year after year,
Exercising discretion that
We took as fear.
Sometimes they fought,
Sometimes they ran,
It was their life—we
Were only hired hands.

Point Man

If only I could see
What lurks behind that tree
Or around the next bend,
  Enemy or friend.
What waits in the grass so thick;
Some harmless creature
Or that sharpened stick.
Focus, if only I can;
My turn almost up,
Who's next—point man.

Womb

Sure passage across
  Monsoon mud,
   Over high ridges,
   Into dark valleys,
Announcing our arrival
For all to hear;
Earth turning,
Grass laid flat,
Not puncture proof
  But thicker than we;
Overburdened, until
We are disgorged
  Without fanfare
  Into the mire.

Its' birth complete,
  Fades into the heavens,
  Quickly,
Leaving us longing
To once again
Enter its'
Trembling belly,
  Lifted away,
  Safe in the womb.

Somewhere Near the Red X

Feet on solid ground.
The jungle quiet, for now,
Preferred over the
   Rotors mournful sound.

Teams forming,
Point man out,
Responding to hurried,
   Whispered shouts.
Going back will be
Better I know,
After we have dealt
   With this foe.

But now, all
Those paddies to cross,
With whispered prayers
For those who surely
   Will be lost.

Goody Drop

Morning,
After a night
Passed with outcry and
Much uproar,
It descends
From the heavens,
Hesitant, then quickly drops
  Into our hell.

Briefly outlined against pale
Daybreak and then
Gone again;
From its bowels
For us fell,
Happiness
In cans of hot chow
And great bags of mail.

Tin Trap

That peanut butter tin
Became a must keepsake,
Not left for the
Surprise Charlie could make.
Never eat it,
Caused too much thirst,
There in the boonies
Nothing worse.
But with it
Those C's you could heat,
By mixing slowly with
A squirt of OD Deet.
Hot chow for
The whole team;
Important then,
Silly as that
May seem;
And
Better to keep
It now than to
Feel it later in our lap,
Among the innards
Of Charlie's booby trap.

Door Gunner

Solitary figure hanging over the
Edge of that vibrating beast as it
Shudders to defy earth's depth of air;
Rushing wind a constant reminder
Of this defiance of nature,
   Laying all below bare.

Gentle bends in trails and
Distant slopes mesmerize while
   soft clouds kiss
And beckon him forward to somersault
Down forever, following the red
Smoking line he has propelled
   Into the mist.

Exposed for all to see, he
Peers down through the hazy heat
While the music of brass clinks
Around his feet;

Guns held by faceless enemies cough
Up into his delicate, dangerous place
From spider holes on the ground;
Only a random chance they will
Hit their mark,
   But death is all around,
   Waiting for a taker.

Medic

Crawling, bag in tow
Through enemies who still litter
This dangerous place he must go,
He moves with single-minded
Purpose from one still figure
To another,
From brother to brother,
Not dwelling on living or dying,
Through the screams and crying.
Working in the
Hot days dusty veil,
With forced patience,
Dispensing his magic
   To relieve their hell.

Medic, sawbones, doc,
Call him what you like,
Always there to answer
In the thick of the fight,
Moving without hesitation,
Through the remnants and brass
Left in the battles aftermath,
While other soldiers pass,
Save those he directs to
Load the bird;
They respond
Without a word
To the soldier, who
Fights a different war,
Knowing
There will come yet more...

Parachute

Floating, suspended
By soft billowy wings,
Held together by only
Silken strings.

Silence, as in a chasm,
Vast, deep, wide;
Billowing canopy,
Rolling, like the tide;
Others like you,
Side by side.

That brief time when
Noise does not exist
And clouds touch
With a soft kiss.

Then, too soon,
Coming quickly,
The ground;
And with it,
    Sound.
Changed,
This warm summer day
And this meadow
Sweet with hay.
No longer a sea of green;
Gone,
    With my collapsing wings..

Duffel Bag

Parting

Standing so quietly that
All around is forgotten.
Time only exists now and
It is slipping away,
With few clues
About the future.

Boy soldiers in the hot sun,
Or gentle snow;
Some in love for the first time,
Or still in love with
His first love,
Standing before him.

Talking in whispered words,
To be recalled again and again;
Reflections later, while the bed
Left is still warm.

Walking away, things said but
Now unable to hear, or say
Back words in the head,
In the heart.
Moving as a sleepwalker who has
Stepped into the night,
Conscious, but not.

What will change in a year?
Will she be here in a year?
Will I
Be
In a year?

Going Over

We were so innocent
Traveling over that vast sea;
Like most, a new, exciting
Experience for me.

The USS Sultan.
Try as we might,
We could not find
Favor in the captains sight.

That sorry ship, reeking
Of us and our smelly boots,
Slick with spilled oil from
Cleaning and cleaning that best
Friend so it would still shoot.

There was a storm, of course,
And the spilling Pacific, so cold
That purple fingers on
Steel rails could hardly hold.

Then, so abruptly deposited
Onto the shores of that strange land,
With hardly a goodbye
Or helping hand,
And
In that sorry place
The next year we would spend,
Unless fate intervened
Before tour's end.

Arrival

Deposited without fanfare
From the great ships hold,
Clutching rope and rifle,
Timing each roll
Lest we slip, fall,
Into the wet cold.

Now the front drops
With a bang into the sand,
At last the feel
Of steady, solid land.

To save, to conquer;
We are here.
But alas,
I hear no cheer.

Temporary I'm sure,
That somber calm,
For we have come
To save Vietnam!

See the End

Get through one day,
Then think about the next,
Always in our mind
Like a hex.

As the tour shortened,
We dwelled on it more,
Thinking of
That friendlier shore.

Then so short, can't
Get in the rack,
But more anxious; maybe
We would get back.

One digit midget, days
From the great silver bird;
Think it, but don't say it;
Bad luck.
    Not a single word.

Mail Call

Easy to tell who did well
  And who appeared
  Under a spell.

Last name called
  And still some linger,
Longing to feel the paper
Between trembling fingers.
Glancing down
  To the ground,
Searching for that
  Not to be found.

Just yesterday, soft
  Words of forever
And now, maybe, her
  Touch again, never.
Seeing her last
  As she turned
And now
  Spurned.

Mail call;
No cookies to share,
  No one to care,
Not even that special one—
  Back there...

Mail—A Good Day

Getting mail now, all these years later
Seems so routine;
Not much excitement about what
Lies within the box, unseen.

But back then, in that land
Way over there,
Mail was hope, fear,
A package of care..

Chow out of a can,
 Okay;
Listening to politicians
With nothing to say,
No problem; but mail call—
Do not delay.

A good day was getting mail,
To hear from anyone at all,
Your name yelled out by
The angel doing mail call.

We all knew who was getting
Mail, who was being let down,
The Dear John from
Some far away town.

Duffel Bag

Private times shared
With each other,
Trouble for me
Trouble for my brother.

For that simple two line note or
Crumpled cookies gone to mold,
In that place, back there, we would
   Give our soul.

Today, sorting through bills,
Tire sales, and such,
I wonder, back then, in that place,
   Would even these trash bound
   Items have meant much.
Probably so, because after all,
A name would have been yelled out
   At mail call...

Books

Those beat up books.
Passed around
One to another.
Paperbacks;
   Most without a cover.

Stuffed in
Pockets, shirts, packs,
Never left unattended
In the rack.
Torn, dog eared;
Muddy,
   Bloody.

Selected pages removed
To be read in solitude
When literary worth
   Bordered on lewd.

Not artistic richness.
No profound truths
   Vomited forth;
Never philosophic doctrine;
   Plain words,
Narrative to free our mind
   Of the here and now;
   To take us from
   That place,
      Somehow.

Black Bart

He could sleep
Anywhere, anytime,
And did.

Humorous with little effort,
Without awareness,
Easy, natural, contagious.
Stress caused calm somehow;
Whether through relentless
Caper or a simple look.

Dirty or tired,
Equally at ease.
Not a leader—more.
Preserving sanity;
   His, ours.

Black Bart.
Every unit had one,
Different name,
Same result;
Helping a bad
Situation seem less so;
Without even knowing it.

Black Bart I love you,
   Wherever you are.

Duffel Bag

DEROS

Daily now I think
How fine,
That land of milk and honey
   And wine;

To see it again.
To be sane
And away from
This place
We cannot tame.

Stay on longer!
So adamant
I refuse,
Though some do,
   To further abuse.

They crave more
   Onslaught,
Heedless of
Lessons taught,
And mindless
   Of fate,
Changing that
DEROS date.

For me, I ask
Only to survive
Till on that great
Shore, I finally arrive,
On time,
   As agreed
Long ago, drunk
   With adventurous greed.

62

Detail

In Vietnam we
Learned to stay out of sight,
While down
   Resting from the fight.

Not from Charlie
Or incoming rounds
Or bursts in the night
And other whistling sounds.

The lessons we learned
While back in the rear,
Darting there
Crouching here,
Was move quick
As you can
When one of your
Buds yelled
   Detail man!

Bound for Heaven

Everyone had those zippo's,
Even if they didn't smoke;
It was expected,
Like asking for a coke.

All had words etched
Into the shiny chrome;
Unit motto, Mom, a girls
Name from back home.

But the phrase most often
Seen stated simply
"bound for heaven,
I've spent my time in hell".
The words seemed to
Free worry, reassure
That all would end well.

Its' author no one knew.
Often the subject of discussion,
But never a clue.

Long after the demise of
Reservoir and flint wheel,
Leaving only a worn shell,
Still we kept it;
    This treasure not for sale:
"bound for heaven,
    I've spent my time in hell".

Short Timer

So short you can't see me.
Days, not weeks, and I am free.

How glorious I begin to feel,
Hot food replacing the OD canned meal.
Not hiding from
The detail man,
Too short, but
Catch me if you can.

A different line of work, no doubt,
Even assembly line widgets,
Things OK to think about
If you are a one digit midget.

No more worry over
Ignition of fuse and primer,
Not for me,
   I'm a short timer!

Things In Our Head

History

It was a long time ago
   Unless
   You're still alive,
Staring into the darkness,
Pissed off,
At something,
Searching for sleep.

Such a long time ago,
But somehow,
   Not.

Shit happens in war.
Things not OK.

Some erupt
With rage
   Or self destruct,
And others never
Really came back.

But most, like me,
Adjust, even though
All of us,
   Through obscene nostalgia
   And ignorant youth
   Never forget.

Strange Thoughts

There were times
In the dark
As sounds rushed through
  The night
That all things
  Seemed right.

Like a spell
Cast by some unseen power
Through my mind
  That fate would be kind.

How strange
It all seems
  Today,
Those thoughts
So out of place

  So far away.

Past

Our desire to be
Gone from that place
Was so great;
That place where daily
We tempted fate.

Now behind us, but
Fate is unkind,
For it is still there,
In our mind.

In that hot hole
We left our soul;
Left forever it seems
To revisit in our dreams.

Now we just
Try to understand
What happened
In that strange land,
And who we became
In all our shame
For others to blame.

In the Rear

Back in the rear
How we amused
Ourselves would sound
Strange to most,
Where things were calmer
And we could coast.

Practical jokes knew
No bounds,
Even between
Incoming rounds.

Somehow, strangely, it
Made normal a
   Situation insane
And brought into
The fold
   Even the most vain.

If you were
The jokes butt,
It didn't matter, you
Knew that, in your gut.

There was no script,
And tongues could not slip
Because all was fair
   From any lip.

Amazing, even with
Newbies after a time,
None without that
Strange sense of humor
   Could you find.

Don't Mean Nuttin'

It don't mean nuttin',
Or so we said,
But 'it' was there,
Somewhere in our head.

All that stuff,
Tucked way in the back,
To preserve sanity;
   Added to the stack.

We wished it away
And moved on
To confront another
Time, alone.

It don't mean nuttin'.
Death was not real,
Filed away in a place
We could not feel.
To survive
   Was the chore.
To live.
   Nothing more.

No room for
Remorse or pain;
Everything to lose
And nothing to gain.

It don't mean nuttin'.
But we knew it did,
And now, often,
It creeps from
　　Under the lid

To remind us
That we are here,
Alive
With nothing more to fear

Except all that stuff,

In there,

　　Year after year.

Who We Were

In that place
For a brief
    Period of time,
We became such
A sorry assortment
    Of mankind;

Reason for our
Quest
Had to wait,
As we chased those
Ghosts in black
Through hell's gate.

Did they understand,
Those who
    Sent us there,
    Through no fault
    Of ours, that
    We could not care.

Students

We lived by listening,
Watching, being lucky.

From old soldiers like Manny
We learned how to survive,
To let pain take care
Of our body while fear
　　Kept us alive.
Respect pain but push
Through it when you must,
　　Manny said;
But always listen to the fear;
Listen closely or be dead.

We existed under
His watchful eye;
He was our pattern
To live and die.

Looking back,
Manny did know best;
Those who understood
And were lucky, survived;
　　Then there were the rest.

Seed

Over there
Across the sea
Is surely still
   A part of me.
Left in lust
Without a thought,
Behind like the dust,
   Taken, but not sought.

In that land
More given than
A hand;

My blood courses
Through another's vein
And weighs heavy
   On my brain.
Were I to blame youth,
Would it be the truth,
I think in dismay
There, so long ago, I lay.

Thoughts I will
   No doubt spend
Now and again
Probably till the very end,

And if one day
The answer is in me,
Will I be
No less
   Still there,
   Across the sea.

Worse Things

There are worse things
  Than dying.

Being forgotten.

You know, by those back there
Who think they understand
What they don't know,
  Can't share.

New buddies are here
But still, somehow
  I am alone,

Wondering if they will remember,
  Those back home;
Or if luck runs out
Will I just be
  Dead and gone.

To be in their thoughts,
  In motion,
Across this vast ocean.

I think it always,

  Please remember I cry;
Otherwise, may
  As well die.

Alike

In some ways we are
Not so different
Than those we stalk;
Sent to do battle
Over things not our fault.

They have loved ones too;
Strange to think,
But of course they do.

Like us, most are young
And away from home;
Not as far,
   But still alone.
We are each others game,
Though for reasons
Not quite the same.

They are quiet, deadly,
Unafraid, because they
   Have been here before;
No choice
In this place of perpetual war.

Always hunted, these little men;
Different enemies, again and again.
Not always right,
But like us, they know
To live
   We must fight.

I hope, for those who die
Someone will cry—

For me as well,
   If it is I.

Hard Lessons

It seemed so easy,
The way they killed us.
Everywhere,
Unless we looked,
   Then nowhere.
So many of us,
So few of them,
Yet
   Everywhere it seemed.

In harmony with
Their land.

Their game
Their rules,
   Everchanging.

They spilled our blood
Drop by caustic drop,
Unrepentive;
We had not a chance.
They knew; but
We learned
   Too late
For
   Too many.

84

Back Home

Where Was the Band

We left without a song
For that land,
   Vietnam.

Some were never there,
But then, who really cared.

The band played for
Those absent without leave,
With families who
   Did not grieve;

Whose ideologies differed
From the
   Greater right
And therefore,
   No reason to fight—

Or was it the
Other way around?
I forget.
Too far away to
   Hear the sound.

Anyway, the truth
Of it I cannot say
For I wrestle my own
Ghosts after the light
   Of each day.

Wounds

Some things I guess
Just never heal.
Even the passage of time
Make them no less real.
Wounds created by fate,
Never to mend—far too late.
It was not the war;
Hell, we don't even know
   What it was for.
Besides, every generation
Has its' war;
It's the politician's whore.
Ours was just so insane.
Marches, Canada, Hanoi Jane.
What to do,
   How to act;
Did they even want
   Us back.
It seems a lifetime
Since we had to go
And whether or not it
Was right, I still don't know.
All those experts think
   Now they see,
But the wound is too deep
   In my brother and me...

Reflection

Jokes about the
'unpopular war',
why we were sent.
We never really knew
What either meant.

Mostly we looked
Into ourselves
And felt nothing
But the urge to go on,
Because each day
Brought us closer
   Home.

Political talk taboo;
And of those who did not come.
Speak only of the future
   So there would be one.

Dirty grinning faces
Hide the fear,
Not of death;
   Being forgotten
By those held dear.
That thought evoking,
In solitude,
   A painful tear.

Our lot was to wonder
Who would care,
When it ended,
If it did,
   And we
   Were still there.

Our Lot

Going off to war
Is the history of man;
Leaving to the waving of
Flags and beating of drums
To meet the enemy in strange lands.

Maybe different for us
Was a country saying go,
But too many people
   Saying no.
All things the same
Except the soldier in
The middle—to blame.

Our lot was a
Return to flags furled,
The silence of drums and
A forever different world.

Back To The World

Back to the world.
Always in our mind.
Waiting for that day,
Putting in our time.

Each day things
Grow more insane
For the pawns in
This political game.

Back in the world
They blame
The warriors for the war,
Those brave youth who
Heeded the call,
    nothing more.

We remind them,
Back in the world, of
Things not right,
Of us and them,
For and against,
Flee or fight.

But still,
    Over here,
Not getting back
To the world
    Is our worst fear...

Bad Things

Zippo Raid

Palms dried
And thatched, woven
On thin bamboo pillars;
No match for
   That chromed menace.
Flick of a thumb
And huts disappear
In a brief
Spiral of smoke;
Never sure,
Enemy or friend,
But a village put to its' end.

Hut to hut,
Giants dizzy with that strange
Mixture of power and sadness
Trod over small gardens,
Then gone,
Leaving behind the heats wavering
Décor and bewilderment,
Standing quietly, unmoving, alone.

Scorched Land

Your scorched land
Will not bloom
At all;
Not any season,
    Spring or fall.

The black of burned
Villages show how
We have wounded you.

Frail papa-son, graven
Faces that betray nothing;
Still, with laden back,
Untiring you go,
Down the jungle track.

The calm walk
Of children,
Tired eyes,
No place to sleep,
Left tearless
To weep.

After we've gone,
Will you still bleed
From our heavy foot
And unwanted seed.

Will you reclaim your land
Laced with powdered brass
Blending into parched grass.
Innocence gone corrupt,
Like a deflated balloon
Trying to blow itself up.

Going Home

Glistening leaves,
Like emeralds,
Such a deep green,
But
Maybe here a spot of red;
And here a creature
Of the jungle,
Tentative,
Raising its dazed head.

In the distance,
Delayed
To the ear,
Raising up, bright,
Napalm,
A blooming chandelier.

Thousands of years
Left alone
In this canopy darkness,
Interrupted by death;
The order of things gone.

Movement. Static.
A moan.
Into the bird.
   Going home.

Final Destination

The dry season.
Choking dust rising,
Settling on those
Black bags
With their lifeless cargo,
While cherry boys
Shuffle by,
Too nervous to
Acknowledge the contents.
Process, then to
The boonies,
For cherry boys
Have much yet
To do,
But these, zipped in the
Endless sound of
   Silence,
Are done,
   Finally,
And homeward bound.

Bad Things

Reaper

Today we all know that
Cloaked figure with
Menacing sickle must
Offer up his bill,
Above prayer and luck,
   Exercising his will.

Impossible not to think about
But the who and when
   Cannot be figured out;
Only the reaper knows, and
We can only wait
To learn which of us has
   Been dealt that hand by fate...

Another Place

The stinging rush of Morpheus,
Nectar lulling me to sleep,
Not yet sunken deep
As my teeming mind
Slowly unwinds
History better left behind.

I'm told I will not grow old
Among those gates of gold
Where reserved for me
A space,
Far away from this place,
Forever to dwell
 Out of this hell.

Rain falling from
A darkened sky
On me lying here,
And others passing by,
Ashamed for being grateful
It is I, not them, to die...

The Cat

Entering that dense
Canopy through splintered trees,
Dark, humid,
Quietened by the planes
Now gone, we stumbled
On to that great beast.
Blood matted fur, his gaze
Tired, holding nothing.
Legs that once stalked
The jungle floor with
Powerful soft strides
Now only twitch, slightly.
As the curtain of his
Eyes slide up, and
We are there, golden limbs tauten;
Sweat stings my eyes
And I blink,
Disturbing the stillness.
A last sigh
And he was gone.
And all that he was.
Forever.

Innocence Gone

So colorful
You were, you are,
Even now, lifeless and torn,
Never again to take flight.

Arbiter of beauty.

Movement quiet as a leaf
Drifting to the ground;
But too delicate
For the roar and rumble
Of that great machine
As it lowered
Ever so slow,
Its' wind grabbing your
Powdered wings before
You could go.

Giver of life
For us, but not you;
Innocence gone,
Without a clue.

Hidden

What hides in
The elephant grass
There
Beyond the great water buffalo.

Does it live
As it waits, or
Is it cold,
Metallic;

Go slow.

Today I am first;
My turn
To find the answer,
To feel the hard learn.

Fate awaits
Me to find,
But
What will
   It be this time.

Not All Bad

Honey Detail

That plume of smoke as
I race toward the latrine
Can only mean
   One thing.

Not mortars, not rockets,
No such luck;
It's the worst detail with
Which a soldier can get stuck.

Smoke black as night—
That's the diesel needed to light;
And the smell;
Something right out of hell—
Yep, it's the unfortunate souls
   On the honey detail.

Ah, that mixture of diesel
And soldierly waste,
About face and move
Away with utmost haste.

The end product of
That outhouse ornate,
Mixed, stirred, and lit
By luckless roster numbers
Picked by cruel fate.

Oh sarge, put me on point
Take all my money,
But please, don't make me
   Burn that honey;

Any bad habit I'll gladly quit-
Just keep me away from those
   Barrels of shit.

Good Things

It was not all bad
In that place.
There were some things
For which one
Developed a taste,
And others with
Some element
Of saving grace;

Not many, to be sure,
But some that offered
Temporary cure.

Neat things to see and do,
But somehow I can't
Recall them,
    Can you?

Important Things

In youth I
Dreamed about things
  I could reap;
Now, all that I
Would gladly let
  Others keep,
But for a pair
Of dry socks, a
  Peaceful nights sleep,
And a hooch that
  Does not leak!

Birthday in the Boonies

Birthday in the boonies,
OD waterproof matches
And C-ration pound cake;
What a celebration it could make.

Small pieces doled out through
Mumbled words, some obscene,
Spoken in that unique
Bush language by fellow warriors,
Rendered in jest, not mean.

Sometimes that crude desert
With flickering matches embedded was
Offered up to shocked surprise
By one close;
  Young, but wise,
With a sheepish grin,
Awkward,
A tribute to his friend.

Through our sweat and stink,
Warm canteens lifted high
For a cheerful drink.

It happened to me,
  And others;
Now, each birthday I
Recall how special that
  Gift from my brothers.

P-38

Oh lord, this
Should not happen
To any man,
Chow break from
That patrol, fruit
Cocktail in hand.
A fine tree
Comforting my back,
The next best thing
To my sack;

And all around me,
Grinning,
Sit my mates,
Because I cannot find
   My P-38...

B-3

Surely I hear the
Trumpets of angels,
And are those raindrop
   Missing me?
Oh glorious day,
That cookie I can clearly see
For I have snagged
The last C-rat B-3.

Sandbags

Shovel man
Bag man
Tie man.
How many bags
Did we fill,
Creating those holes,
Leveling that hill.

I believe it safe to say
That every soldier
Got to play;
Shovel man
Bag man
Tie man,
   You and the sand.

Bags of burlap
Or nylon
Filled with the
Sand of Vietnam.
On them we sat,
Behind them we huddled
And across them we walked
To avoid those puddles.

We left and they stayed,
   Those bags,
Though surely now
They are tattered rags.
It's there too,
   The sand.
Not in the same place,
But there, scattered over that strange
land.
Shovel man
Bag man
Tie man. You and the sand.

Surprise

What a pleasant surprise
To this tired ear,
Noise so low I
Can hardly hear.
A great script
This day has wrote;
The platoon sergeant
Has a sore throat!

Beating the Draft

It was Jerry's idea
To beat the draft.
Lets just join and
Have the last laugh.

So instead of the standard
Two, we took four;
No U.S. for us;
Regular Army Corps.

Better training this
Way says he;
What the hell
Says dummy me.

As I look back, I
Guess there was some bonus,
It was ten months rather
Than six before we left CONUS.

Same destination,
Different time;
Free stamps, and
The occasional mine.

But finally, we left there,
Except as my buds went
To long hair
And civilian rags,
Dummy me went to
Fort by God Bragg!

Well we did beat the
Draft, so it's all moot,
Although often I still wonder how
Jerry's ass would fit my boot!

Whoops

Oh what I would
Give on these
Nice little hikes
If just once I
Could cross a
Rice paddy without
Slipping off the dike!

Kilroy

Kilroy was there,
In that land of thick
Jungle and red dirt.
I never saw him,
But I did see his work.

Everywhere.

On sandbag walls,
Caps and helmets,
Outhouse stalls,
Once on a rifle butt
And all over every Quonset hut.

I am certain there was only one
Because each autograph
Had the same face,
And none would erase.

He must be ancient;
His mark was seen
Back in the big war;
Kilroy gets around,
That's for sure.

I don't know who he is,
Or why he does it, but
His work always provoked a grin,
And the next time we're called,
I know he will be there again.

Kilroy — every soldiers friend.

Finally

Lost Ideals

Too many of us were
Leaders too young to lead,
And soldiers too full
Of adventure and then
Of bitterness over
   Ideals unfulfilled.
Our knowledge of the
World was torn
Away and replaced with
Thoughts of only surviving.
Life in that place was
   Trying to stay sane.
Somehow,
The great adventure
   Went awry
And with it the
   Best of our youth.

Memorial Day

Somber faces
Reflect much, but
Little.
Things known
But not understood;
Too hard to tell
Even if they could.
Embedded forever,
Burned deep,
Escaping
Only in sleep.
Flags rustle
Evoking memories
Long pushed rear;
Down worn faces
A tear,
Speeches falling
On deaf ears,
Like so many
Leaves falling silently
To ground,
Noted, but without a sound.
Here for reasons
Too hard to explain
Through the
Anguish and pain.
When the music
Dies and others leave,
Only they are left, alone,
To grieve.

For Brian

Brian talked of writing a book.
Small talk, as soldiers do,
But it was his dream.

While all of us were searching
For answers, or understanding,
But finding neither,
Brian was stringing words
Together in his mind,
To be spewed forth years
Later in not one, but
Many books.

We did not perish over there
And that caused us to smile
As we left,
Though not the same as
A year before;
But there was a rip in fate
And a part of that place
Entered Brian, extracting its'
Toll these many years later.

Brian is gone, but
His dreams, in those books,
Are not.

You did it Brian.

127

Remember

Think of them
If not often,
  Now and then.
Keep a special
Place within
For who they were,
  What they did.

In the eyes of your child
Remember those whose
Children cry for
Fathers
  Too young to die;
For those
Still among you,
Feel their scars
And recall why.

Know that all you
Do and see,
For those thousands
  Will never again be.

In that black wall
Do not appall;
Learn enough
From each faceless name
  To know your shame;
And
If you forsaked
Them then,
  Remember today,
For it was not their sin
That sent them to that place
  So far away.

Today and Beyond

Acknowledge the past and
From it learn
But for its offerings
Do not yearn.

   It is today we must begin
And not be cheated by
Dwelling on
   Things that were then.

Past tears and happiness have a place
In dreams
   To point the way,
   But belong
Far behind the
   Certainty and desire of today.

Now is a chance with each
Sunset to be reborn,
Just as the fire circles
And returns
   As it surely will
     Each morn.

CPSIA information can be obtained
at www.ICGtesting.com
Printed in the USA
BVHW040824230520
580190BV00015B/882